Dogs & Puppies
IN CROSS STITCH

Lynne Porter

MEREHURST

THE CHARTS

Some of the designs in this book are very detailed and, due to inevitable space limitations, the charts may be shown on a comparatively small scale; in such cases, readers may find it helpful to have the particular chart with which they are currently working enlarged.

THREADS

The projects in this book were all stitched with DMC stranded cotton embroidery threads. The keys given with each chart also list thread combinations for those who wish to use Anchor or Madeira threads. It should be pointed out that the shades produced by different companies vary slightly, and it is not always possible to find identical colours in a different range.

First published in 1996 by Merehurst Limited
Ferry House, 51-57 Lacy Road, Putney, London SW15 1PR
Copyright © 1996 Merehurst Limited
ISBN 1 85391 453 3

A catalogue record for this book is available from the British Library.

Edited by Heather Dewhurst
Designed by Maggie Aldred
Photography by Marie-Louise Avery
Illustrations by John Hutchinson (pp5-7) and King & King (p30)
Typesetting by Dacorum Type & Print, Hemel Hempstead
Colour separation by Fotographics Limited, UK – Hong Kong
Printed in Hong Kong by Wing King Tong

Merehurst is the leading publisher of craft books and has an excellent range of titles to suit all levels. Please send to the address above for our free catalogue, stating the title of this book.

CONTENTS

Introduction   4

Basic Skills   4

Mille-Fleurs Footstool   8

Baby Bib, Mug and Placemat   12

Key Box and Key Rack   16

Set of Coasters   20

Fireside Cushions   24

Washdays' Peg Bag   28

Clothes Brush and Towel   32

Autumn Harvest Picture   36

Acknowledgements & Suppliers   40

INTRODUCTION

Cross stitch is a very old form of needlework, and is a part of embroidery heritage in countries as far apart as the Netherlands, Mexico and China. Design motifs have been exchanged between cultures and several design elements are now common to several cultures.

Cross stitch was often used to decorate household items such as linen and clothes, and is still used today for this purpose. However, with the increasing popularity of cross stitch in recent times, it is now possible to find a wide variety of products in which to mount your embroidery, such as clothes brushes or glass coasters.

Dogs are often known as 'man's best friend', and what better subject can there be than an appealing dog or puppy? In this book dogs and puppies are portrayed on a wide range of specially created projects, which include a footstool, key box, clothes brush, towel and many more, and which vary in difficulty from the very simple to the more challenging and demanding ones.

All the designs have been worked on the ever-popular Aida fabric, but this could be replaced with any evenweave fabric of a suitable count. Cross stitch is extremely easy to do and, with help from the Basic Skills section of this book, even complete beginners will find many of the designs well within their scope.

I hope that you enjoy selecting and stitching the items in this book as much as I enjoyed designing and making them. Whatever your level of skill, and whichever projects you choose, you can look forward to many happy hours of stitching.

BASIC SKILLS

BEFORE YOU BEGIN

PREPARING THE FABRIC
Even with an average amount of handling, many evenweave fabrics tend to fray at the edges, so it is a good idea to overcast the raw edges, using ordinary sewing thread, before you begin.

THE INSTRUCTIONS
Each project begins with a full list of the materials that you will require; Aida is a fabric produced by Zweigart. Note that the measurements given for the embroidery fabric include a minimum of 3cm (1½in) all around to allow for stretching it in a frame and preparing the edges to prevent them from fraying.

Aida fabric is woven in blocks. Work each cross stich over one block of fabric. Each square of the chart represents one block of fabric, and each symbol on the chart represents a single cross stitch, its colour indicated by the symbol used. Start the cross stitch embroidery at the centre of the design unless otherwise indicated, working all cross stitches so that the top stitches always lie in the same direction.

Colour keys for stranded embroidery cottons – DMC, Anchor or Madeira – are given with each chart. It is assumed that you will need to buy one skein of each colour mentioned in a particular key, even though you may use less, but where two or more skeins are needed, this information is included in the main list of requirements.

To work from the charts, particularly those where several symbols are used in close proximity, some readers may find it helpful to have the chart enlarged so that the squares and symbols can be seen more easily. Many photocopying services will do this for a minimum charge.

Before you begin to embroider, always mark the centre of the design with two lines of basting stitches, one vertical and one horizontal, running from edge to edge of the fabric, as indicated by the arrows on the charts.

As you stitch, use the centre lines given on the chart and the basting threads on your fabric as reference points for counting the squares and threads to position your design accurately.

WORKING IN A HOOP

A hoop is the most popular frame for use with small areas of embroidery. It consists of two rings, one fitted inside the other; the outer ring usually has an adjustable screw attachment so that it can be tightened to hold the stretched fabric in place. Hoops are available in several sizes, ranging from 10cm (4in) in diameter to quilting hoops with a diameter of 38cm (15in). Hoops with table stands or floor stands attached are also available.

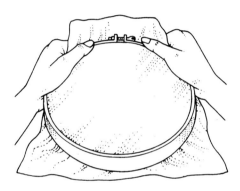

1 To stretch your fabric in a hoop, place the area to be embroidered over the inner ring and press the outer ring over it, with the tension screw released. Tissue paper can be placed between the outer ring and the embroidery, so that the hoop does not mark the fabric. Lay the tissue paper over the fabric when you set it in the hoop, then tear away the central embroidery area.

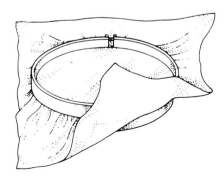

2 Smooth the fabric and, if necessary, straighten the grain before tightening the screw. The fabric should be evenly stretched.

WORKING IN A RECTANGULAR FRAME

Rectangular frames are more suitable for larger pieces of embroidery. They consist of two rollers, with tapes attached, and two flat side pieces, which slot into the rollers and are held in place by pegs or screw attachments. Available in different sizes, either alone or with adjustable table or floor stands, frames are measured by the length of the roller tape, and range in size from 30cm (12in) to 68cm (27in).

As alternatives to a slate frame, canvas stretchers and the backs of old picture frames can be used. Provided there is sufficient extra fabric around the finished size of the embroidery, the edges can be turned under and simply attached with drawing pins (thumb tacks) or staples.

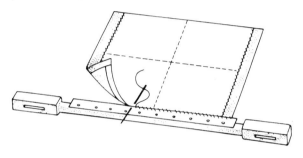

1 To stretch your fabric in a rectangular frame, cut out the fabric, allowing at least an extra 5cm (2in) all around the finished size of the embroidery. Baste a single 12mm (½in) turning on the top and bottom edges and oversew strong tape, 2.5cm (1in) wide, to the other two sides. Mark the centre line both ways with basting stitches. Working from the centre outwards and using strong thread, oversew the top and bottom edges to the roller tapes. Fit the side pieces into the slots, and roll any extra fabric on one roller until the fabric is taut.

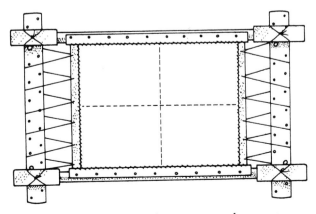

2 Insert the pegs or adjust the screw attachments to secure the frame. Thread a large-eyed needle (chenille needle) with strong thread or fine string and lace both edges, securing the ends around the intersections of the frame. Lace the webbing at 2.5cm (1in) intervals, stretching the fabric evenly.

EXTENDING EMBROIDERY FABRIC

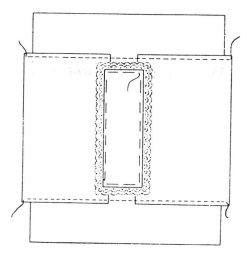

It is easy to extend a piece of embroidery fabric, such as a bookmark, to stretch it in a hoop.

● Fabric oddments of a similar weight can be used. Simply cut four pieces to size (in other words, to the measurement that will fit both the embroidery fabric and your hoop) and baste them to each side of the embroidery fabric before stretching it in the hoop in the usual way.

THE STITCHES

BACKSTITCH

Backstitch is used in the projects to give emphasis to a particular foldline, an outline or a shadow. The stitches are worked over the same number of threads

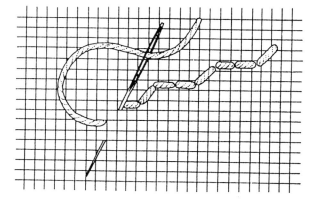

as the cross stitch, forming continuous straight or diagonal lines.

● Make the first stitch from left to right; pass the needle behind the fabric and bring it out one stitch length ahead to the left. Repeat and continue in this way along the line.

CROSS STITCH

For all cross stitch embroidery, the following two methods of working are used. In each case, neat rows of vertical stitches are produced on the back of the fabric.

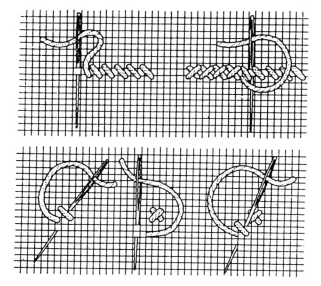

● When stitching large areas, work in horizontal rows. Working from right to left, complete the first row of evenly spaced diagonal stitches over the number of threads specified in the project instructions. Then, working from left to right, repeat the process. Continue in this way, making sure each stitch crosses in the same direction.
● When stitching diagonal lines, work downwards, completing each stitch before moving to the next.

FINISHING

TO BIND AN EDGE

1 Open out the turning on one edge of the bias binding and pin in position on the right side of the fabric, matching the fold to the seamline. Fold over the cut end of the binding. Finish by overlapping the starting point by about 12mm (½in). Baste and machine stitch along the seamline.

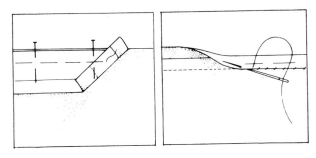

2 Fold the binding over the raw edge to the wrong side, baste and, using matching sewing thread, neatly hem to finish.

PIPED SEAMS

Contrasting piping adds a special decorative finish to a seam and looks particularly attractive on items such as cushions and cosies.

You can cover piping cord with either bias-cut fabric of your choice or a bias binding: alternatively, ready covered piping cord is available in several widths and many colours.

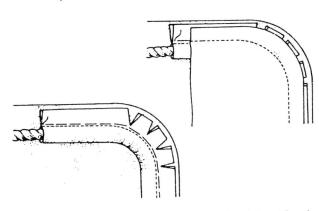

1 To apply piping, pin and baste it to the right side of the fabric, with seam lines matching. Clip into the seam allowance where necessary.

2 With right sides together, place the second piece of fabric on top, enclosing the piping. Baste and then either hand stitch in place or machine stitch, using a zipper foot. Stitch as close to the piping as possible, covering the first line of stitching.

3 To join ends of piping cord together, first overlap the two ends by about 2.5cm (1in). Unpick the two cut ends of bias to reveal the cord. Join the bias

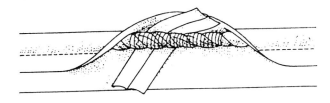

strip as shown. Trim and press the seam open. Unravel and slice the two ends of the cord. Fold the bias strip over it, and finish basting around the edge.

MOUNTING EMBROIDERY

The cardboard should be cut to the size of the finished embroidery, with an extra amount added all round to allow for the recess in the frame.

LIGHTWEIGHT FABRICS

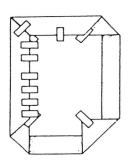
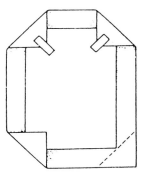

1 Place embroidery face down, with the cardboard centred on top, and basting and pencil lines matching. Begin by folding over the fabric at each corner and securing it with masking tape.

2 Working first on one side and then the other, fold over the fabric on all sides and secure it firmly with pieces of masking tape, placed about 2.5cm (1in) apart. Also neaten the mitred corners with masking tape, pulling the fabric tightly to give a firm, smooth finish.

HEAVIER FABRICS

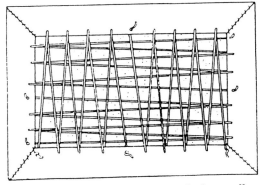

● Lay the embroidery face down, with the cardboard centred on top; fold over the edges of the fabric on opposite sides, making mitred folds at the corners, and lace across, using strong thread. Repeat on the other two sides. Finally, pull up the stitches fairly tightly to stretch the fabric firmly over the cardboard. Overstitch the mitred corners.

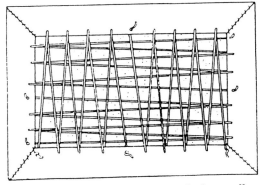

7

Mille-Fleurs Footstool

This elegant footstool would make a delightful and useful addition to a home, and could well become a talking point when guests come to call. The design is based on Flemish tapestries of the 16th century, mille-fleurs meaning 'many flowers'.

MILLE-FLEURS FOOTSTOOL

YOU WILL NEED

For the Footstool, with an inner frame measurement of 30cm × 38cm (12in × 15¼in), and design area of 20cm × 28cm (8in × 11¼in), or 144 stitches by 198 stitches:

50cm × 58cm (20in × 23¼in) of navy, 18-count Aida fabric
Stranded embroidery cotton in the colours given in the panel
No26 tapestry needle
Footstool (for suppliers, see page 40)
50cm × 58cm (20in × 23¼in) of navy, lightweight cotton fabric, for lining (optional)
Matching sewing thread
Strong thread, for lacing across the back

●

THE EMBROIDERY

Prepare the fabric, basting the central horizontal and vertical design lines, and stretch it in a frame, following the instructions on page 5. Start the embroidery at the centre of the design, using two strands of thread in the needle, and stitching over one block of fabric. Gently steam press the finished embroidery on the wrong side.

MAKING UP THE FOOTSTOOL

If the footstool pad is covered with pale fabric, it will be necessary to line the embroidery before making up the footstool. With right sides together and matching edges, pin and baste the lining fabric to the embroidery. Taking a 12mm (½in) seam allowance, stitch around the sides leaving a 15cm (6in) opening in the middle of one side. Trim the corners. Turn the embroidery right-side out, slip stitch the opening to secure, and press. If lining is unnecessary, turn a 12mm (½in) hem on the embroidered fabric.

Undo the screws of the footstool base. Mark the centre sides of the pad and the embroidery with pins. Matching the centre points, and checking that the design is centred on the top of the pad, lace in position as illustrated on page 7. Replace the pad in the footstool base and tighten the screws.

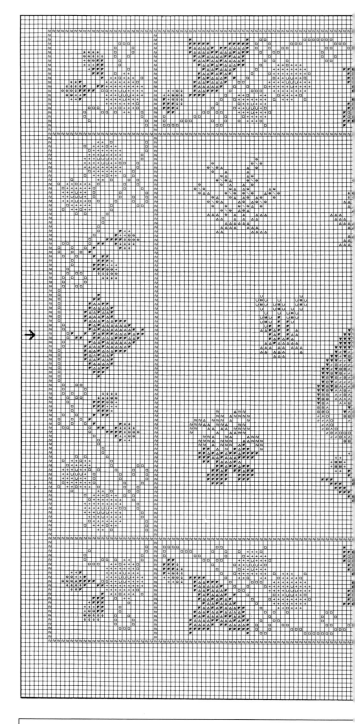

MILLE-FLEURS FOOTSTOOL ▲		DMC	ANCHOR	MADEIRA
▼	Dark tan	420	375	2104
⊘	Medium tan	3828	373	2103
8	Light tan	422	367	2102
∧	Dark honey	3046	887	2206
O	Light honey	3047	852	2205
+	Cream	712	926	1707
■	Black	310	403	Black

		DMC	ANCHOR	MADEIRA			DMC	ANCHOR	MADEIRA
▬	Red	321	13	0510	☐	Medium green	988	257	1402
⊞	Dark yellow	725	297	0108	△	Light green	989	256	1401
U	Yellow	726	295	0109	⟍	White	White	2	White
→	Blue	334	977	1003	⊖	Medium pink	352	9	0303
ℵ	Light blue	3325	144	1002	⧚	Dark pink	350	11	0213
1	Very light blue	775	975	1001					
⤶	Dark green	987	258	1403					

Bib, Mug and Placemat

The naughty puppy who decorates these delightful items will bring a smile to any child's face. These three projects would make ideal presents for a new member of the family.

BIB, MUG AND PLACEMAT

YOU WILL NEED

For the Bib, with a design area of 5cm × 7.5cm (2in × 3in), or 27 stitches by 42 stitches:

Purchased bib (for suppliers, see page 40)
Stranded embroidery cotton in the colours given
in the appropriate panel
No24 tapestry needle

For the Mug, with a single design area of 6.5cm × 5cm (2½in × 2in), or 34 stitches by 27 stitches:

Purchased Stitch-a-Mug (for suppliers, see page 40)
Stranded embroidery cotton in the colours given in
the appropriate panel
No24 tapestry needle

For the Placemat, measuring 42.5cm × 29cm (17in × 11½in), with a design area of 22cm × 5cm (8½in × 2in), or 120 stitches by 29 stitches:

44cm × 30cm (17½in × 12in) of sky blue, 14-count
Aida fabric
Stranded embroidery cotton in the colours given
in the appropriate panel
No24 tapestry needle
2m (2¼yd) of blue bias binding, 2.5cm (1in) wide
Matching sewing thread

•

THE BIB AND MUG

For the bib, mark the central horizontal and vertical design lines with basting stitches and stretch the bib in a frame, following the instructions on page 5. Start the embroidery at the centre of the design, using three strands of thread in the needle for the cross stitch, and two strands of thread for the backstitch.

For the mug, the vinyl strip measuring 25cm × 9cm (10in × 3½in) should meet where the handle is attached. You can centre the design on the vinyl strip and stitch it once, or stitch the design twice so that it can be seen on each side of the mug. If you stitch the design twice, measure 7cm (2¾in) from each end of the strip and baste vertically, to give the vertical centre design lines. Start the embroidery in the centre of the design, using two strands of

thread in the needle. When complete, slip the strip back into the mug and snap the inner shell back into place.

THE PLACEMAT

Prepare the edges of the fabric and mark the central vertical design line of the fabric with basting stitches. Measure 9cm (3½in) up from the bottom (long edge) of the fabric and baste for the central horizontal design line. Stretch the fabric in a frame, following the instructions on page 5. Start the embroidery at the centre of the design, using two strands of thread in the needle for the cross stitch and one strand for the backstitch. Gently steam press the finished embroidery on the wrong side.

To round off the corners of the fabric, place a cup against each corner and lightly mark the fabric with a pencil. Trim off the excess corner fabric. Pin, baste, and machine stitch the bias binding to the wrong side of the fabric, matching raw edges. Fold the bias binding to the right side and carefully topstitch in position. Press the completed placemat.

PLACEMAT ▼		DMC	ANCHOR	MADEIRA
◤	Dark brown	434	310	2009
⊖	Medium brown	436	363	2011
◳	Honey	739	368	2014
◿	White	White	2	White
◼	Black	310	403	Black
▬	Green	368	214	1310
+	Light green	369	213	1309

Note: bks outlines in medium brown.

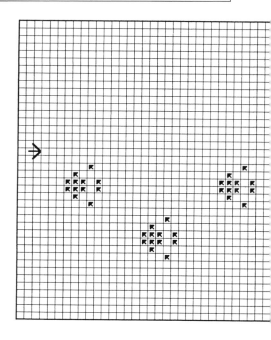

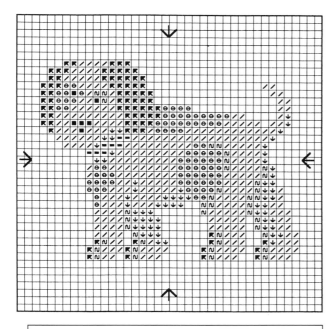

BIB ▼

		DMC	ANCHOR	MADEIRA
⬈	Dark brown	434	310	2009
⊖	Medium brown	436	363	2011
ℕ	Honey	739	368	2014
∕	White	White	2	White
■	Black	310	403	Black
▬	Green	368	214	1310
＋	Light green	369	213	1309

Note: bks outlines in medium brown.

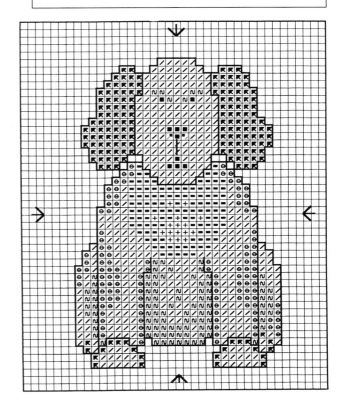

MUG ▲

		DMC	ANCHOR	MADEIRA
⬈	Dark brown	434	310	2009
⊖	Medium brown	436	363	2011
ℕ	Light brown	437	362	2012
↓	Honey	738	361	2013
∕	Light honey	739	368	2014
■	Black	310	403	Black
▬	Green	368	214	1310

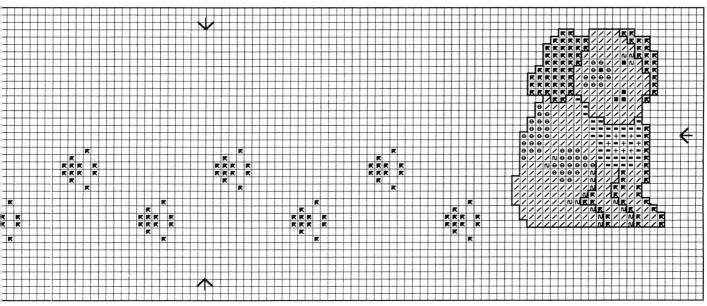

Key Box
and
Key Rack

If you are forever misplacing your keys, this key box and rack could provide the ideal solution to the problem, while making a delightful addition to your home.

KEY BOX
AND KEY RACK

YOU WILL NEED

For the Key Box, with a working area of
20cm × 25cm (8in × 10in), and a design area
of 12.5cm × 17.5cm (5in × 7in), or
71 stitches by 98 stitches:

28cm × 33cm (11¼in × 13¼in) of cream,
14-count Aida fabric
Stranded embroidery cotton in the colours given
in the appropriate panel
No26 tapestry needle
Purchased key box (for suppliers, see page 40)
21.5cm × 26.5cm (8½in × 10½in) of iron-on
interfacing (optional)
Strong thread, for lacing across the back

For the Key Rack, with a working area of
10cm × 10cm (4in × 4in), and a design area
of 7cm × 7.5cm (2¾in × 3in), or
49 stitches by 56 stitches:

19cm × 19cm (7½in × 7½in) of sky blue,
18-count Aida fabric
Stranded embroidery cotton in the colours given
in the appropriate panel
No26 tapestry needle
Purchased key rack (for suppliers, see page 40)
12cm × 12cm (4¾in × 4¾in) of iron-on
interfacing (optional)
Strong thread, for lacing across the back

•

THE EMBROIDERY

Prepare the edges of the fabric, and baste the central horizontal and vertical design lines. Stretch the fabric in a frame, following the instructions on page 5. For the key box, start the embroidery just left of centre, on the dog's head, counting carefully to ensure correct placement. Use two strands of thread in the needle for the cross stitch and one strand for the backstitch. Complete the bottom left area of the design, then carefully count up and across to continue on the top right of the design. For the key rack, start the embroidery in the centre. Gently steam press the finished embroideries on the wrong side.

MAKING UP

You can either lace the embroidery over the card provided by the manufacturer, or use iron-on interfacing as described below. For both items, mark the centre lines on the card template provided. If you prefer to use iron-on interfacing, lightly mark the centre lines with pencil on the back of the embroidery and on the interfacing, and remove the basting stitches. Iron a piece of interfacing to the back of each embroidery, aligning the pencil marks. If you are not using interfacing, leave the basting stitches in at this stage.

To complete the assembly of both the key box and key rack, lay the embroidery face-down with the template on top then, matching centre lines, draw around the template using a soft pencil. Draw a second line about 4cm (1½in) outside the first line and cut along this outer line. For the key box, lace as shown on page 7. To lace the key rack, make a line of running stitches about 2cm (¾in) in from the raw edge, following the marked line. Place the card on the wrong side and pull up the thread, spacing the gathers evenly. Secure the gathering thread. Lace the back of the embroidery in a clockwise fashion, starting at 12, then down to 6, back to 1, and then down to 7, etc. If using interfacing, carefully cut out the embroidery along the template pencil line, and complete the assembly.

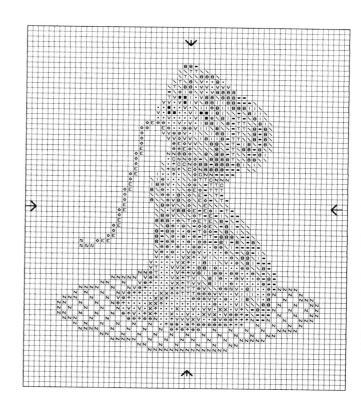

KEY RACK ◄	DMC	ANCHOR	MADEIRA
I Very light tan	3776	347	2302
◤ Light tan	301	349	2306
8 Medium tan	400	351	2305
▬ Dark tan	300	352	2304
T Very dark tan	801	359	2007
• White	White	2	White
V Cream	746	926	0101
X Dark cream	677	886	2207
⊖ Beige	739	368	2014
■ Black	310	403	Black
N Blue	793	131	0911
C Dark blue	797	132	0912
N Light gold	3047	852	2205
↑ Dark gold	3046	887	2206
◇ Green	988	257	1402
E Dark green	987	258	1403

KEY BOX ▲	DMC	ANCHOR	MADEIRA
1 Very light tan	3776	347	2302
◤ Light tan	301	349	2306
8 Medium tan	400	351	2305
▬ Dark tan	300	352	2304
T Very dark tan	801	359	2007
• White	White	2	White
V Cream	746	926	0101
X Dark cream	677	886	2207
⊖ Beige	739	368	2014
■ Black	310	403	Black
▲ Warm brown	838	380	1914
N Blue	793	131	0911
C Dark blue	797	132	0912
N Gold	3047	852	2205
↑ Dark gold	3046	887	2206

Note: bks dog in very light tan, and bird and tree in warm brown.

Set of Coasters

These attractive coasters would make ideal gifts for dog lovers. They can be used for drinks glasses or for small items on a dressing table, and make presents which are both decorative and functional.

SET OF COASTERS

YOU WILL NEED

For each Coaster, with a working area of 7.5cm (3in)
in diameter and a design area of 5cm (2in),
or German Shepherd 38 stitches by 38 stitches,
Spaniel 33 stitches by 35 stitches, and
Rough Collie 35 stitches by 39 stitches:

15cm (6in) square of cream, 18-count Aida fabric
Stranded embroidery cotton in the colours given
in the appropriate panel
No26 tapestry needle
15cm (6in) square of iron-on interfacing
Glass coaster (for suppliers, see page 40)

●

THE EMBROIDERY

Prepare the edges of the fabric and mark the central
vertical and horizontal design lines with basting
stitches. Stretch the fabric in a frame, following the
instructions on page 5. Start the embroidery at the
centre of the design, using two strands of thread in
the needle. Gently steam press the finished embroidery on the wrong side.

MAKING UP

Remove the basting stitches and iron the interfacing
to the wrong side of the embroidery. Lay the embroidery face-down on a flat surface and, using the paper
template provided with the coaster, draw around the
design, ensuring that it is central. Check that the
template line is correct by laying the coaster over
the top, and then carefully cut out the circle. Place
the embroidery face-down in the recess on the base
of the coaster, place the paper template on top of the
reverse side of the embroidery, then peel the backing
from the protective base and carefully place it over
the back of the coaster, ensuring that the embroidery
and paper template remain in position.

SPANIEL ▼		DMC	ANCHOR	MADEIRA
⊡	Dark brown	938	380	2005
⊞	Dark tan	433	358	2008
⬩	Medium tan	434	310	2009
S	Light tan	435	365	2010
◁	Very light tan	436	363	2011
→	Dark beige	437	362	2012
V	Medium beige	738	361	2013
+	Light beige	739	366	2014
■	Black	310	403	Black
▬	Grey	646	8581	1812
◣	Very light grey	3072	847	1805

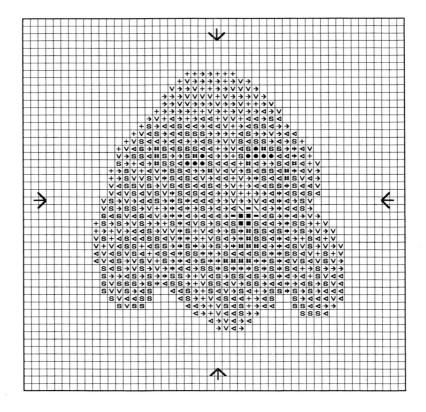

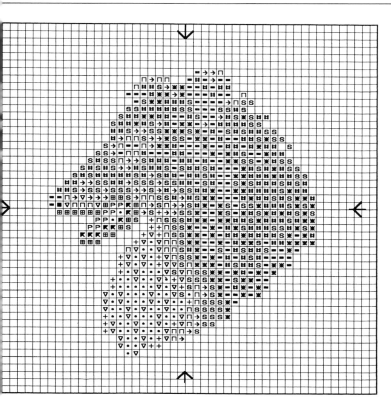

ROUGH COLLIE ◀		DMC	ANCHOR	MADEIRA
•	White	White	2	White
P	Dark pink	221	896	0811
▬	Very dark brown	938	380	2005
✳	Dark brown	801	359	2007
⊞	Dark tan	433	358	2008
S	Medium tan	435	365	2010
→	Light tan	436	363	2011
⊓	Dark honey	738	361	2013
+	Honey	739	366	2014
▽	Light grey	3072	847	1805
⊞	Medium grey	647	8581	1813
◣	Dark grey	844	401	1810
■	Black	310	403	Black

GERMAN SHEPHERD ▶		DMC	ANCHOR	MADEIRA
◥	Beige pink	950	4146	2309
+	Light pink	224	894	0813
P	Dark pink	223	895	0812
✳	Dark brown	801	359	2007
⊓	Very light tan	738	361	2013
→	Light tan	437	362	2012
◪	Medium tan	436	363	2011
S	Dark tan	435	365	2010
•¦•	Very dark tan	434	310	2009
▽	Light grey	648	900	1814
•	White	White	2	White
⊞	Dark grey	646	8581	1812
◣	Very dark grey	844	401	1810
■	Black	310	403	Black

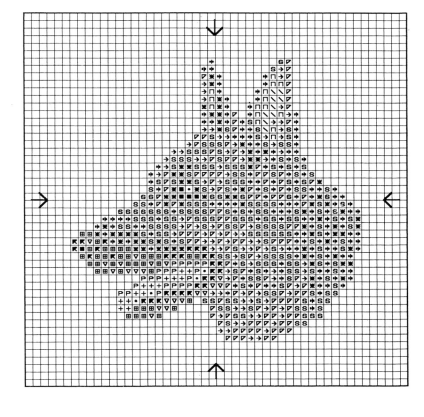

Fireside Cushions

This delightful pair of cushions with their amusing scenes show puppies snoozing in front of the fire. These bright and cheerful cushions will bring warmth to any room, and would look delightful decorating a child's bedroom.

FIRESIDE CUSHIONS

YOU WILL NEED

For each Cushion, measuring 30cm (12in) square
excluding edging, with a design area of
16cm × 14cm (6³/₈in × 5¹/₂in), or
89 stitches by 77 stitches:

35cm (14in) square of cream, 14-count Aida fabric
Stranded embroidery cotton in the colours given
in the panel
No26 tapestry needle
33cm (13¹/₄in) square of fabric, for cushion back
Matching sewing thread
Cushion pad, 28cm (11¹/₄in) in diameter
2m (2¹/₄yd) of contrasting cushion cord, 6mm
(¹/₄in) in diameter

THE EMBROIDERY

Prepare the edges of the fabric and mark the central horizontal and vertical design lines with basting stitches. Stretch the fabric in a frame, following the instructions on page 5. Start the embroidery at the centre of the design, using two strands of cotton in the needle for the cross stitch and one strand for the backstitch. Gently steam press the finished embroidery on the wrong side.

MAKING UP

For each cushion cover, trim the embroidered fabric to measure 33cm (13¹/₄in) square, keeping the design central. Remove the basting stitches. With right sides together, place the backing fabric on to the embroidered fabric, baste and machine stitch around the sides, leaving a 20cm (8in) opening in the middle of one side. Trim the corners and turn the cover right side out. Insert the cushion pad and slip stitch the opening to secure. To complete the cover, slip stitch cord around the edges.

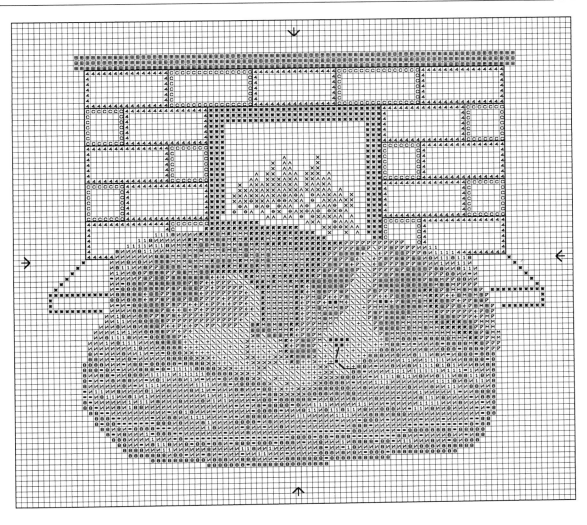

LABRADOR ◄		DMC	ANCHOR	MADEIRA
■	Black	310	403	Black
▛	Very dark brown	3371	381	2004
⊞	Dark tan	434	310	2009
M	Medium tan	436	363	2011
▽	Light tan	437	362	2012
←	Beige	738	361	2013
⊖	Dark grey	645	400	1811
▬	Dark blue	312	979	1005
8	Medium blue	322	978	1004
ɴ	Light blue	3755	161	1013
1	Very light blue	775	975	1001
✳	Gold	3046	887	2206
∧	Orange	977	313	2307
X	Yellow	743	305	0113
I	Dark brown	839	380	1913

BEAGLE ▲		DMC	ANCHOR	MADEIRA
■	Black	310	403	Black
▛	Very dark brown	3371	381	2004
M	Dark tan	433	358	2008
⊞	Medium tan	435	365	2010
▽	Light tan	437	362	2012
←	Beige	739	366	2014
◸	White	White	2	White
⊖	Dark grey	646	8581	1812
+	Very light grey	3072	847	1805
▬	Dark blue	312	979	1005
8	Medium blue	322	978	1004
ɴ	Light blue	3755	161	1013
1	Very light blue	775	975	1001
⊳	Medium grey	648	900	1814
✳	Gold	3046	887	2206
C	Light brick	402	368	2301
4	Dark brick	3776	347	2302
∧	Orange	977	313	2307
X	Yellow	743	305	0113

Note: bks dog's nose in black, and bricks in gold.

Washdays' Peg Bag

These naughty puppies playing havoc with the washing will bring a touch of sunshine to any washday, and make a delightful and amusing embroidery to decorate this practical peg bag.

WASHDAYS' PEG BAG

YOU WILL NEED

For the Peg Bag, measuring 30cm × 35cm (12in × 14in) excluding coat hanger hook, with a design area of 21.5cm × 15cm (8¼in × 6in), or 120 stitches by 86 stitches:

Two pieces of 30cm × 23cm (12in × 9¼in) cream, 14-count Aida fabric
Stranded embroidery cotton in the colours given in the panel
No26 tapestry needle
Cotton Perlé thread, DMC 436 or equivalent, for washing line
29cm × 21.5cm (11½in × 8¾in) of lightweight iron-on interfacing
2.5m (2½yd) of contrasting bias binding, 2.5cm (1in) wide
Matching sewing thread
30cm × 35cm (12in × 14in) of heavy cotton fabric, for backing
Coat hanger, 28cm (11¼) wide
50cm (20in) of ribbon, 10mm (⅜in) wide, to match bias binding

•

THE EMBROIDERY

Taking one of the pieces of Aida fabric, prepare the edges and mark the central horizontal and vertical design lines with basting stitches. Stretch the fabric in a frame, following the instructions on page 5. Start the embroidery at the centre of the design, using two strands of thread in the needle for the cross stitch, and one strand for the backstitch. When the backstitching is complete, use the Cotton Perlé thread to straight stitch the washing line. Gently steam press the finished embroidery on the wrong side.

MAKING UP

Remove the basting stitches from the embroidered fabric. Place the fabric and interfacing wrong sides together, and iron the interfacing in place. Attach the bias binding to the top edge, pin, baste, and machine stitch to the wrong side of the fabric, matching raw edges. Fold the binding to the right side and topstitch in position. Take the second piece of unstitched Aida fabric and make a double

12mm (½in) hem along one long edge (this is the bottom edge). Lay the piece of heavy cotton fabric backing, right side down, on a flat surface, lay the unembroidered piece of Aida fabric over this, right side up, matching top edges, and pin in position. Mark the centre position of the coat hanger hook with a basting stitch. Place the embroidered Aida, right side up, on top of both the backing fabric and the unembroidered Aida section, and align with the bottom edges of the backing fabric. Pin in position.

To round off the corners of the fabric, place a cup against each corner and lightly mark the fabric with a pencil. Trim off the excess corner fabric. Baste *all* layers together. Add the bias binding all the way around, as described above, leaving a small opening for the coat hanger hook. Topstitch the bias binding from the right side, carefully following the edge, and leaving the opening for the hook. Press the completed peg bag. Slip the coat hanger inside the top section and up through the opening. To finish, add a ribbon bow.

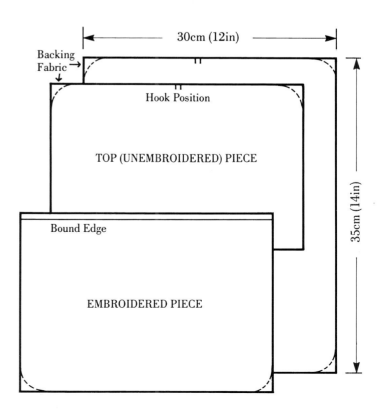

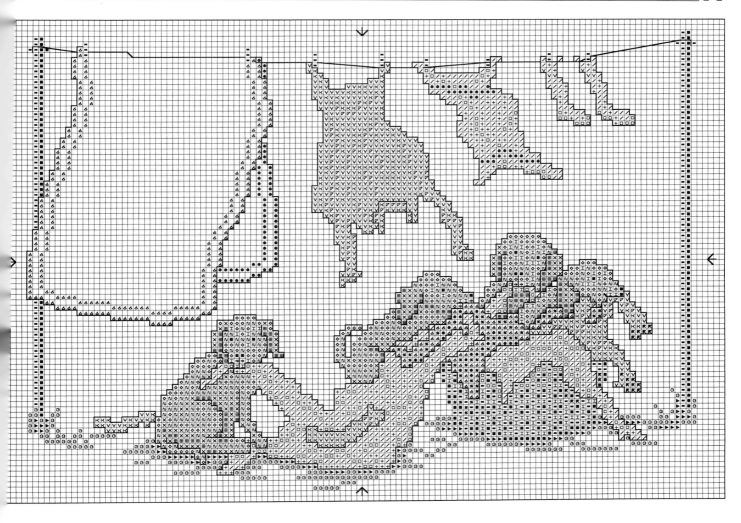

WASHDAYS' PEG BAG ▲		DMC	ANCHOR	MADEIRA
I	Ivory	822	390	1908
◇	Cream	739	366	2014
∩	Caramel	738	361	2013
X	Medium caramel	437	362	2012
⊞	Dark caramel	436	363	2011
■	Brown	869	944	2105
■	Dark brown	3031	360	2003
□	Grey	415	398	1803
V	Light blue	3755	161	1013
⊼	Very dark blue	312	979	1005
K	Medium blue	334	977	1003
6	Light pink	761	8	0404
•	Dark pink	3712	10	0406

		DMC	ANCHOR	MADEIRA
⊠	Medium pink	760	9	0405
G	Medium green	3347	266	1408
▶	Dark green	3345	268	1406
⊿	Dark blue	322	978	1004
◦|•	Beige	841	378	1911
∕	White	White	2	White
+	Very light grey	762	397	1804
	Medium grey*	318	398	1802

Note: bks pink washing with medium pink, blue washing with dark blue, white washing with medium grey, and puppies with dark caramel (*used for backstitch only).*

Clothes Brush and Towel

This clothes brush and towel, with the design of cute and cuddly West Highland Whites and Scottish Terriers, would make a lovely addition to any bathroom.

CLOTHES BRUSH AND TOWEL

YOU WILL NEED

For the Clothes Brush, with a working area of
15cm × 3cm (6in × 1¼in), and a design area
of 12.5cm × 2cm (5in × ¾in), or
88 stitches by 14 stitches:

*23cm × 11.5cm (9¼in × 4½in) of sky blue,
18-count Aida fabric
Stranded embroidery cotton in the colours given in
the appropriate panel
No26 tapestry needle
18cm × 6cm (7¼in × 2⅜in) of lightweight iron-on
interfacing
Purchased clothes brush (for suppliers,
see page 40)*

For the Towel, with a working area of
27cm × 6.5cm (10¾in × 2½in), and a design area
of 18cm × 4cm (7¼in × 1½in):

*Purchased towel, measuring 28cm × 46cm
(11in × 18in) (for suppliers, see page 40)
Stranded embroidery cotton in the colours given in
the appropriate panel
No26 tapestry needle*

•

THE EMBROIDERY

For the clothes brush, prepare the edges of the fabric
and mark the central horizontal and vertical design
lines with basting stitches. Stretch the fabric in a
frame, following the instructions on page 5. Start the
embroidery at the centre of the design, using two
strands of thread in the needle for the cross stitch,
and one strand for the backstitch.

For the towel, baste the central horizontal and
vertical design lines of the Aida area and stretch it
in a frame. Start the embroidery at the centre of the
design, using three strands of thread in the needle
for the cross stitch, and one strand for the backstitch. Gently steam press the finished embroideries
on the wrong side.

MAKING UP

For the clothes brush, remove the basting stitches
and iron the interfacing to the wrong side of the
embroidery. Placing the acetate inset from the top of
the brush over the embroidery, draw around the

inset, ensuring that the design is central. Carefully
cut out the embroidery. Replace the acetate in the
brush, and place the embroidery on top, with the
right side facing the acetate. Re-assemble the brush
top. Using a small hammer, with a soft piece of cloth
covering the hammer-head to protect the brush rim,
tap the nails into the wood.

To complete the towel, simply remove the basting
stitches.

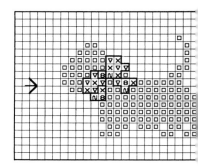

TOWEL ▼		DMC	ANCHOR	MADEIRA
■	Black	310	403	Black
□	White	White	2	White
X	Red	817	47	0211
8	Green	989	256	1401
▽	Blue	798	131	0911
Ⅳ	Yellow	726	295	0109

*Note: bks bow outlines on black dogs in white, and bow outlines on
white dogs in black.*

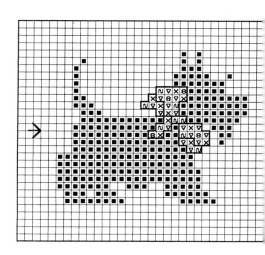

CLOTHES BRUSH ▼		DMC	ANCHOR	MADEIRA
■	Black	310	403	Black
□	White	White	2	White
X	Red	817	47	0211
8	Green	989	256	1401
▽	Blue	798	131	0911
Ν	Yellow	726	295	0109

Note: bks bow outlines on black dogs in white, and bow outlines on white dogs in black.

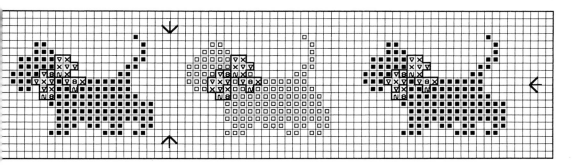

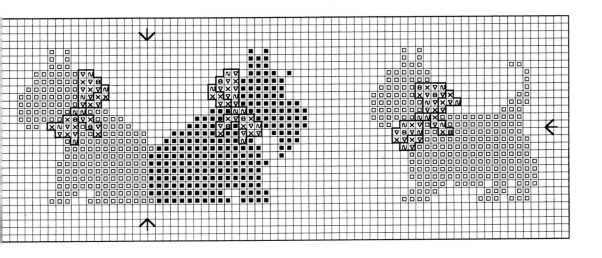

Autumn Harvest Picture

This delightful picture with its adorable puppy sitting in a basket would certainly appeal to any dog-lover, and receive a place of honour in any room in the home.

AUTUMN HARVEST PICTURE

YOU WILL NEED

For the Picture, with a design area of
16.5cm (6½in) square, or 93 stitches by
90 stitches:

25cm (10in) square of peach, 14-count Aida fabric
Stranded embroidery cotton in the colours given
in the panel
No26 tapestry needle
Strong thread, for lacing across the back
Card to fit frame recess, for mounting
Frame of your choice

●

THE EMBROIDERY

Prepare the fabric, and mark the central horizontal
and vertical design lines with basting stitches.
Sretch the fabric in a frame, following the
instructions on page 5. Start the embroidery at the
centre of the design, using two strands of thread in
the needle for the cross stitch, and one strand for
the backstitch. Gently steam press the finished
embroidery on the wrong side, leaving the basting
stitches in position.

MOUNTING

Use either of the methods described on page 7 to
lace and mount your finished embroidery. To achieve
a smooth finish, you may find it helpful to pin the
fabric to the edge of the board, to hold it in place.
Starting at the centre of each side, push the pins into
the board edge, stretching the fabric gently as you
go. Check that the grain of the fabric is straight, and
the embroidery is central, before lacing or fixing
with tape. Place the stretched embroidery in the
frame of your choice. If the frame has glass, use a
mount or place thin strips of card inside the frame
rebate to prevent the embroidery touching the glass.
As well as spoiling the look of the embroidery,
condensation might form on the inside of the glass
and cause mildew stains on your precious work.

AUTUMN HARVEST PICTURE ▶		DMC	ANCHOR	MADEIRA
■	Black	310	403	Black
↖	Very dark grey	844	401	1810
⊖	Dark grey	645	400	1811
△	Medium grey	647	8581	1813
L	Light grey	648	900	1814
1	Very light grey	3072	847	1805
╱	White	White	2	White
•	Very dark tan	801	359	2007
▬	Dark tan	433	358	2008
●|●	Medium tan	435	365	2010
◇	Beige	739	366	2014
⋒	Light peach	3779	868	0404
X	Medium peach	758	9575	0403
⋈	Dark peach	3778	337	0402
U	Light tan	437	362	2012
H	Light green	472	253	1414
→	Medium green	471	265	1501
8	Dark green	470	266	1502
M	Dark pink	351	10	0214
+	Grey/beige	3782	388	1907

Note: bks leaf veins in very dark tan.

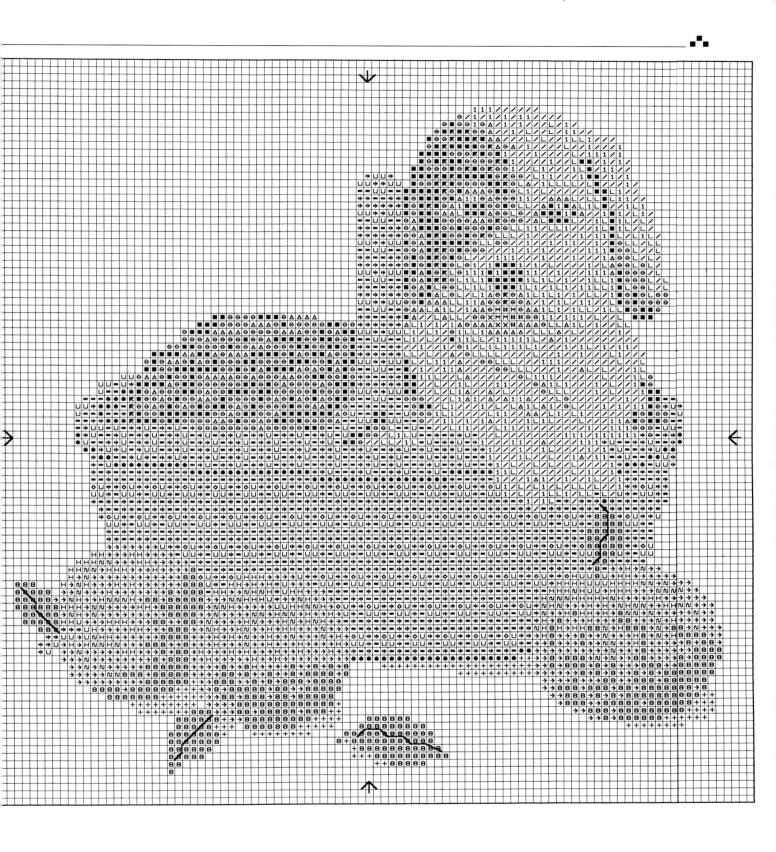

ACKNOWLEDGEMENTS

The author would like to thank the following people for their help with this book:

Pat Bell, Jenny Burns, Jenny Cartwright, Shirley Crosswaite, Gill Slone,
Sheila Stiff and Joanne Swain.

Thanks are also due to Cara Ackerman of DMC Creative World Ltd, for supplying the fabric and threads; Sarah Gray of Framecraft Miniatures Ltd, for supplying the clothes brush and glass coasters; Ian & Joan Foster of Remember When, for supplying the footstool, key box and key rack; and Karen Finch of Crafty Ideas, for supplying the towel, bib and Stitch-a-Mug. When writing to any supplier, please include a stamped, self-addressed envelope for your reply.

Finally, I would like to express my thanks to my husband and daughter, for their help, support and encouragement.

Embroidery kits designed by Lynne Porter may be obtained from her company:
Lynne Porter Designs, 2 Fourth Avenue, Bridlington, East Yorkshire YO15 2LN

SUPPLIERS

Crafty Ideas
The Willows
Cassington Road
Eynsham
Oxford OX8 1L

Remember When
Cheriton Cottage
Wreningham
Norwich NR16 1BE

The following mail order company has supplied some of the basic items needed for making up the projects in this book:

Framecraft Miniatures Limited
372-376 Summer Lane
Hockley
Birmingham B19 3QA
England
Telephone: 0121 359 4442

Addresses for Framecraft stockists worldwide

Ireland Needlecraft Pty Ltd
2-4 Keppel Drive
Hallam, Victoria 3803
Australia

Danish Art Needlework
PO Box 442, Lethbridge
Alberta T1J 3Z1
Canada

Sanyei Imports
PO Box 5, Hashima Shi
Gifu 501-62
Japan

The Embroidery Shop
286 Queen Street
Masterton
New Zealand

Anne Brinkley Designs Inc.
246 Walnut Street
Newton
Mass. 02160
USA

S A Threads and Cottons Ltd.
43 Somerset Road
Cape Town
South Africa

For information on your nearest stockist of embroidery cotton, contact the following:

DMC
(also distributors of Zweigart fabrics)

UK
DMC Creative World Limited
62 Pullman Road
Wigston
Leicester LE8 2DY
Telephone: 0116 811040

USA
The DMC Corporation
Port Kearney Bld.
10 South Kearney
N.J. 07032-0650
Telephone: 201 589 0606

AUSTRALIA
DMC Needlecraft Pty
P.O. Box 317
Earlswood 2206
NSW 2204
Telephone: 02599 3088

MADEIRA
UK
Madeira Threads (UK) Limited
Thirsk Industrial Park
York Road, Thirsk
N. Yorkshire YO7 3BX
Telephone: 01845 524880

USA
Madeira Marketing Limited
600 East 9th Street

Michigan City
IN 46360
Telephone: 219 873 1000

AUSTRALIA
Penguin Threads Pty Limited
25-27 Izett Street
Prahran
Victoria 3181
Telephone: 03529 4400

COATS AND ANCHOR
UK
Coats Paton Crafts
McMullen Road
Darlington
Co. Durham DL1 1YQ
Telephone: 01325 381010

USA
Coats & Clark
P.O. Box 27067
Dept CO1
Greenville
SC 29616
Telephone: 803 234 0103

AUSTRALIA
Coats Patons Crafts
Thistle Street
Launceston
Tasmania 7250
Telephone: 00344 4222